Bond

Non-verbal Reasoning

Assessment Papers

7–8 years

Andrew Baines

Nelson Thornes

Text © Andrew Baines 2003, 2007
Original illustrations © Nelson Thornes Ltd 2003, 2007

The right of Andrew Baines to be identified as author of this work has
been asserted by him in accordance with the Copyright, Designs and Patents
Act 1988.

All rights reserved. No part of this publication may be reproduced or
transmitted in any form or by any means, electronic or mechanical,
including photocopy, recording or any information storage and retrieval
system, without permission in writing from the publisher or under licence from
the Copyright Licensing Agency Limited, of Saffron House, 6–10 Kirby Street,
London, EC1N 8TS.

Any person who commits any unauthorised act in relation to this publication
may be liable to criminal prosecution and civil claims for damages.

First edition published in 2003 by:
Nelson Thornes Ltd

Second edition published in 2007 by:
Nelson Thornes Ltd
Delta Place
27 Bath Road
CHELTENHAM
GL53 7TH
United Kingdom

13 / 10 9 8 7 6 5 4 3 2

A catalogue record for this book is available from the British Library

ISBN 978 1 4085 1717 8

Illustrations by Nigel Kitching
Page make-up by Wearset Ltd

Printed in China by 1010 Printing International Ltd

Before you get started

What is Bond?

This book is part of the Bond Assessment Papers series for non-verbal reasoning, which provides a **thorough and continuous course in non-verbal reasoning** from ages six to twelve. It builds up non-verbal reasoning skills from book to book over the course of the series.

What does this book cover?

Non-verbal reasoning questions can be grouped into four distinct groups: identifying shapes, missing shapes, rotating shapes, coded shapes and logic. This book lays the early foundations through practice of six different question types: finding the odd one out, completing a visual sequence, completing a picture, completing a visual analogy, reflections and hidden shapes. All the questions at this level involve pictures so that they are similar to the picture puzzles with which children may already be familiar. Later in the series pictures will be replaced by shapes.

The age given on the cover is for guidance only. As the papers are designed to be reasonably challenging for the age group, any one child may naturally find him or herself working above or below the stated age. The important thing is that children are always encouraged by their performance. Working at the right level is the key to this.

What does the book contain?

- **8 papers** – each one contains 30 questions.

- **Scoring devices** – there is a scoring box at the end of each paper and a Progress Chart at the back. The chart is a visual and motivating way for children to see how they are doing. Encouraging them to colour in the chart as they go along and to try to beat their last score can be highly effective!

- **Next Steps** – advice on what to do after finishing the papers can be found on the inside back cover.

- **Answers** – located in an easily-removed central pull-out section.

How can you use this book?

One of the great strengths of Bond Assessment Papers is their flexibility. They can be used at home, school and by tutors to:

- provide regular non-verbal reasoning practice in **bite-sized chunks**

- **highlight strengths and weaknesses** in the core skills

- identify **individual needs**

- set **homework**

- set **timed formal practice** tests – allow about 30 minutes.

It is best to start at the beginning and work though the papers in order.

What does a score mean and how can it be improved?

If children colour in the Progress Chart at the back, this will give an idea of how they are doing. The Next Steps inside the back cover will help you to decide what to do next to help a child progress. We suggest that it is always valuable to go over any wrong answers with children.

Don't forget the website . . . !

Visit www.bond11plus.co.uk for lots of advice, information and suggestions on everything to do with Bond, helping children to do their best, and exams.

Paper 1

Which is the odd one out? Circle the letter.

Example

6

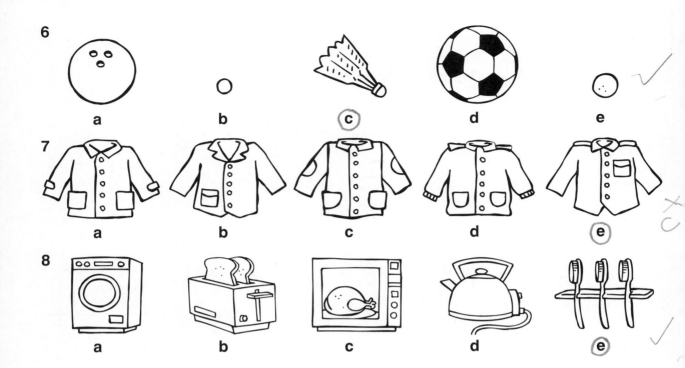

a   b   (c)   d   e

7

a   b   c   d   (e)

8

a   b   c   d   (e)

Which one comes next? Circle the letter.

Example

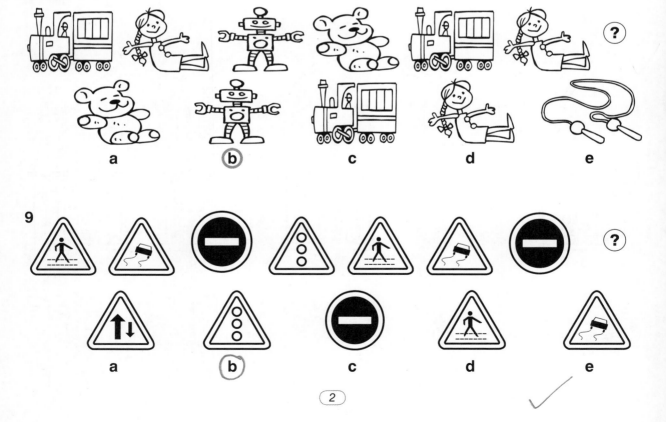

a   (b)   c   d   e

9

a   (b)   c   d   e

2

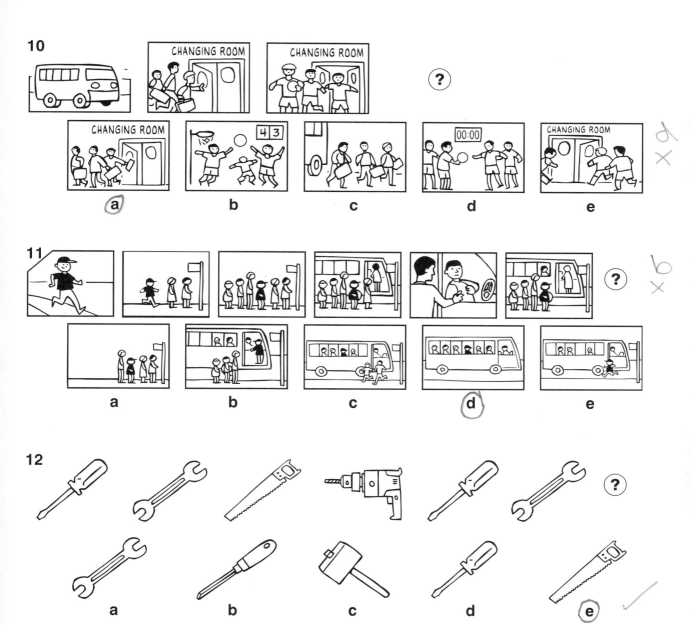

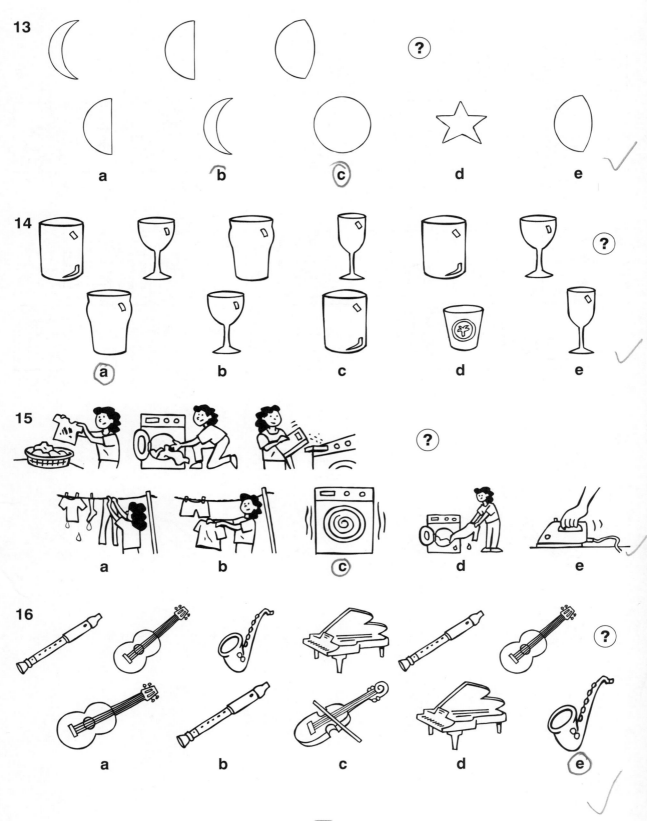

Which picture completes the second pair in the same way as the first pair?
Circle the letter.

Example

17

18

19

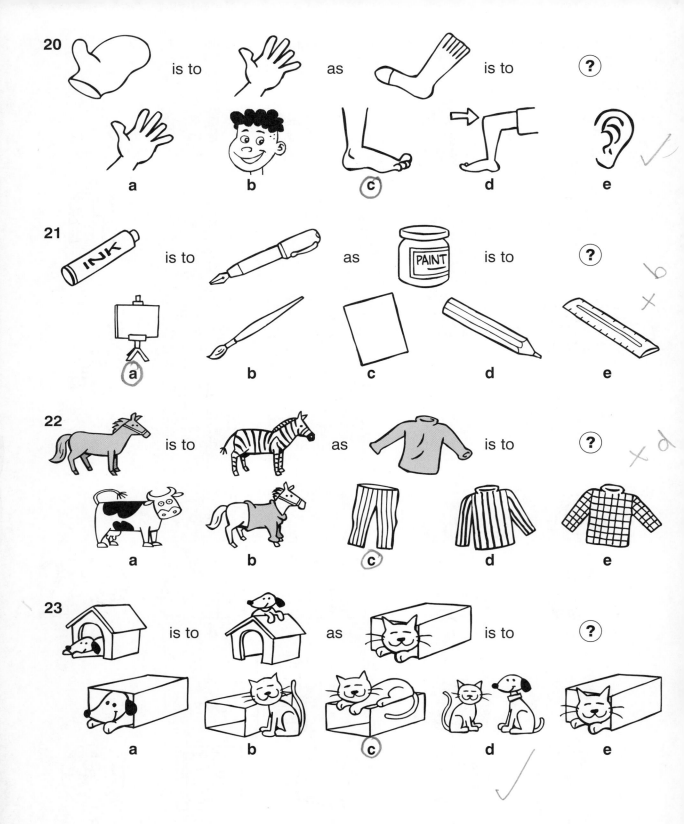

20 is to   as   is to   **?**

a   b   c   d   e

21 is to   as   is to   **?**

a   b   c   d   e

22 is to   as   is to   **?**

a   b   c   d   e

23 is to   as   is to   **?**

a   b   c   d   e

24

a   b   c   d   e ✓

In which larger picture is the smaller picture hidden? Circle the letter.

Example

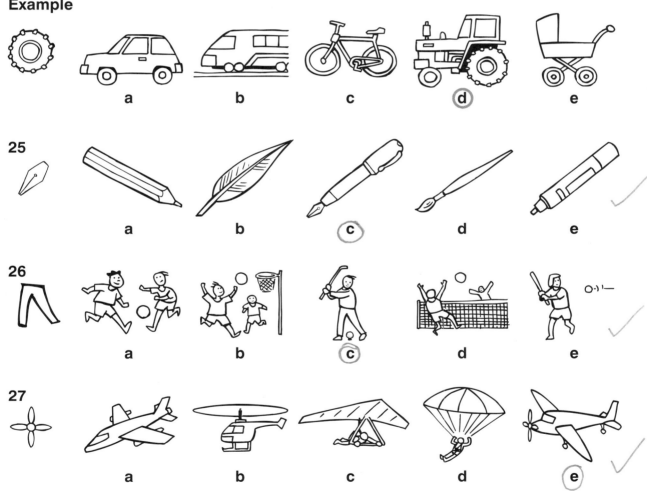

a   b   c   d   e

25   a   b   c   d   e ✓

26   a   b   c   d   e ✓

27   a   b   c   d   e ✓

Which picture on the right is the reflection of the picture given on the left, in the dotted mirror line? Circle the letter.

Example

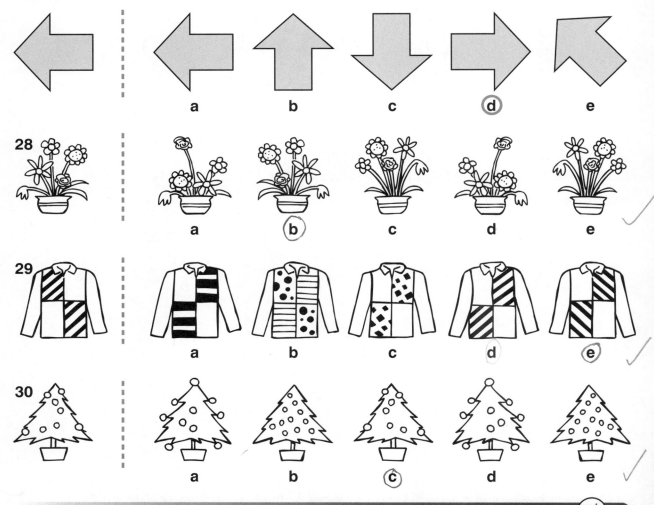

Paper 2

Which is the odd one out? Circle the letter.

Example

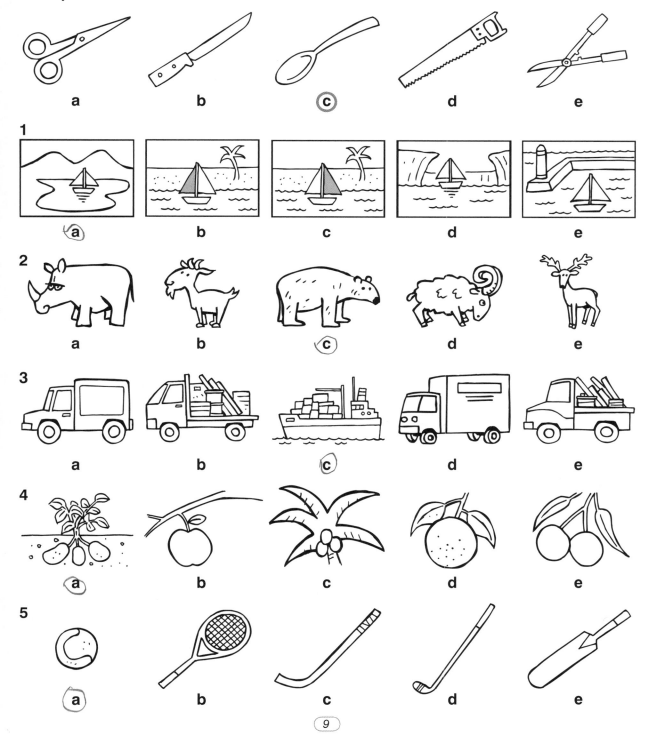

a   b   c   d   e

1

a   b   c   d   e

2

a   b   c   d   e

3

a   b   c   d   e

4

a   b   c   d   e

5

a   b   c   d   e

6

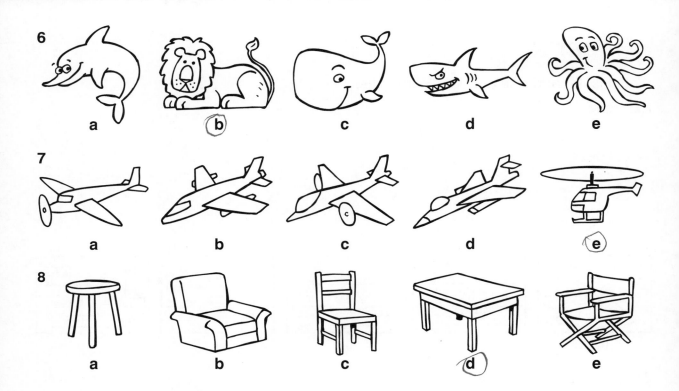

a   b   c   d   e

7

a   b   c   d   e

8

a   b   c   d   e

Which one comes next? Circle the letter.

Example

a   b   c   d   e

9

?

a   b   c   d   e

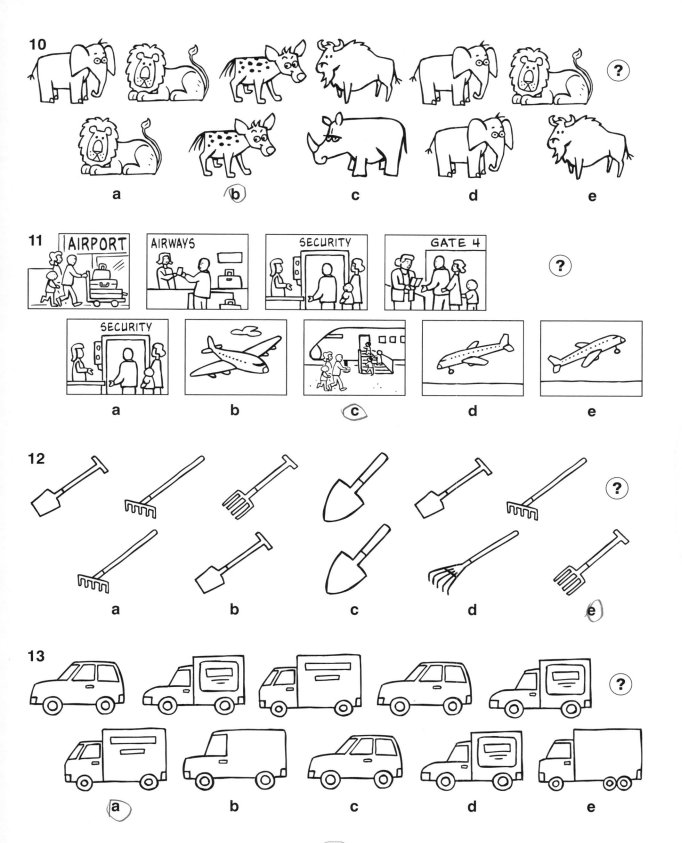

10

a b c d e

11

AIRPORT AIRWAYS SECURITY GATE 4

a b c d e

12

a b c d e

13

a b c d e

14

a b c d e

15

a b c d e

16

a b c d e

Which picture completes the second pair in the same way as the first pair?
Circle the letter.

Example

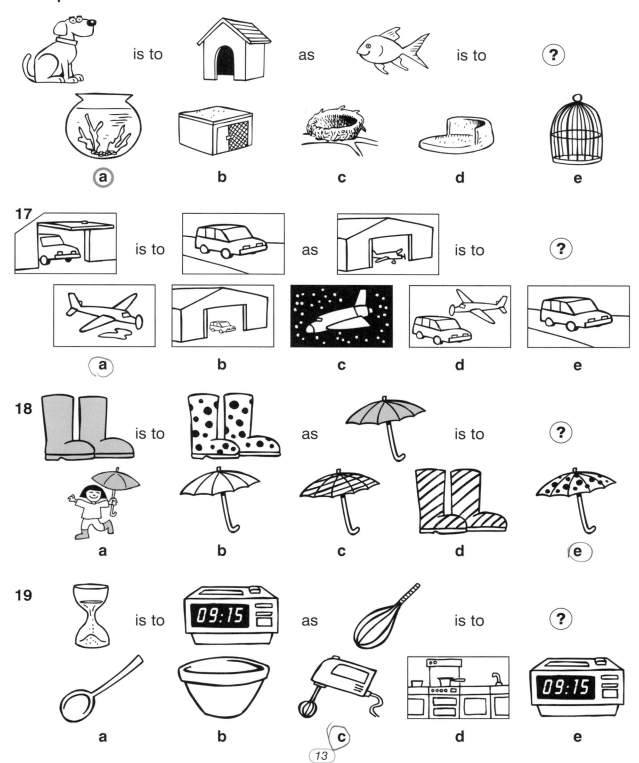

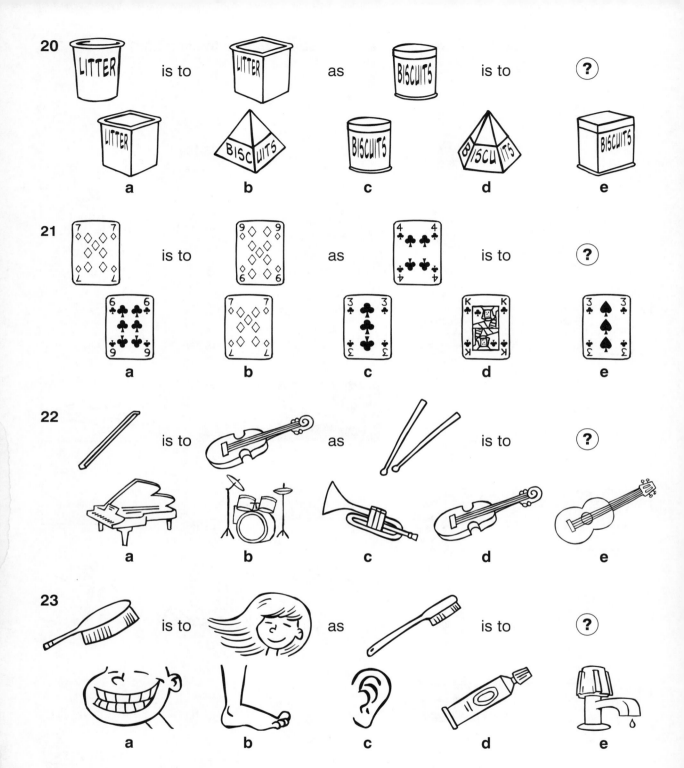

20 LITTER is to LITTER as BISCUITS is to **?**
a b c d e

21 [card] is to [card] as [card] is to **?**
a b c d e

22 [violin bow] is to [violin] as [drumsticks] is to **?**
a b c d e

23 [brush] is to [head] as [toothbrush] is to **?**
a b c d e

24

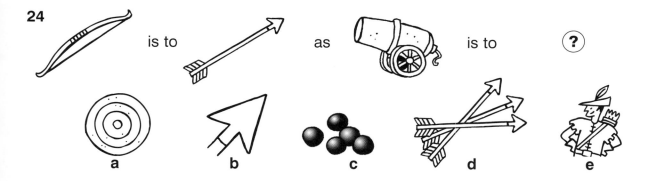

Which picture on the right is the reflection of the picture given on the left, in the dotted mirror line? Circle the letter.

Example

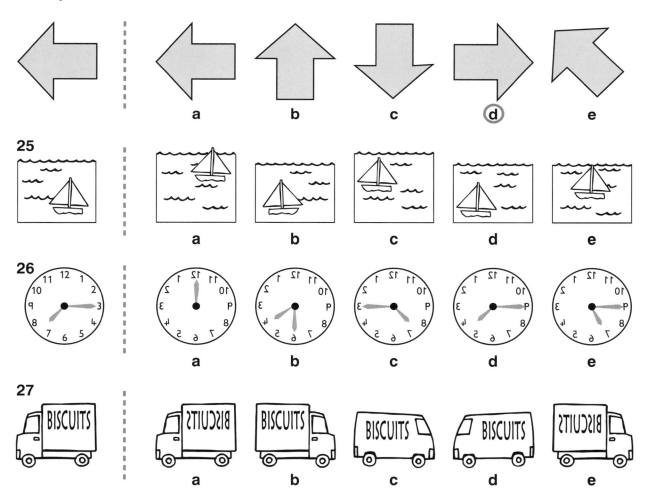

Which shape or picture completes the larger square? Circle the letter.

Example

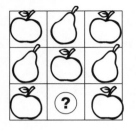

a

b

ⓒ

d

e

28

a

b

c

d

e

29

a

b

c

d

e

30

a

b

c

d

e

Now go to the Progress Chart to record your score!   Total   30

Paper 3

Which is the odd one out? Circle the letter.

Example

6

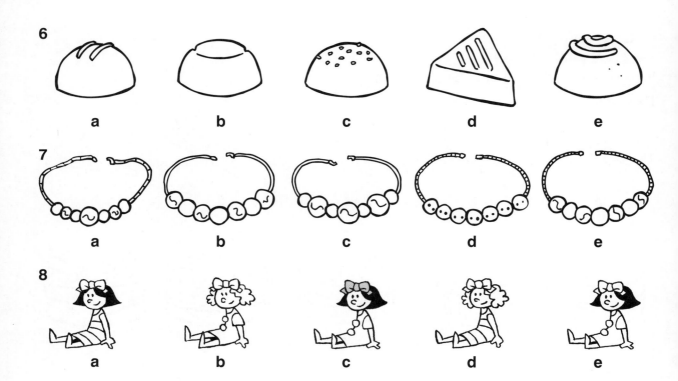

7

8

a b c d e

Which one comes next? Circle the letter.

Example

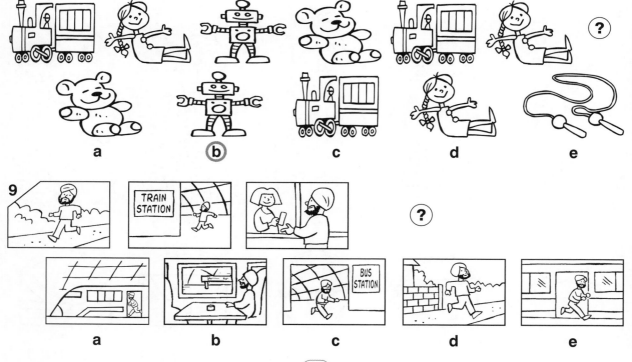

a **b** c d e

9

a b c d e

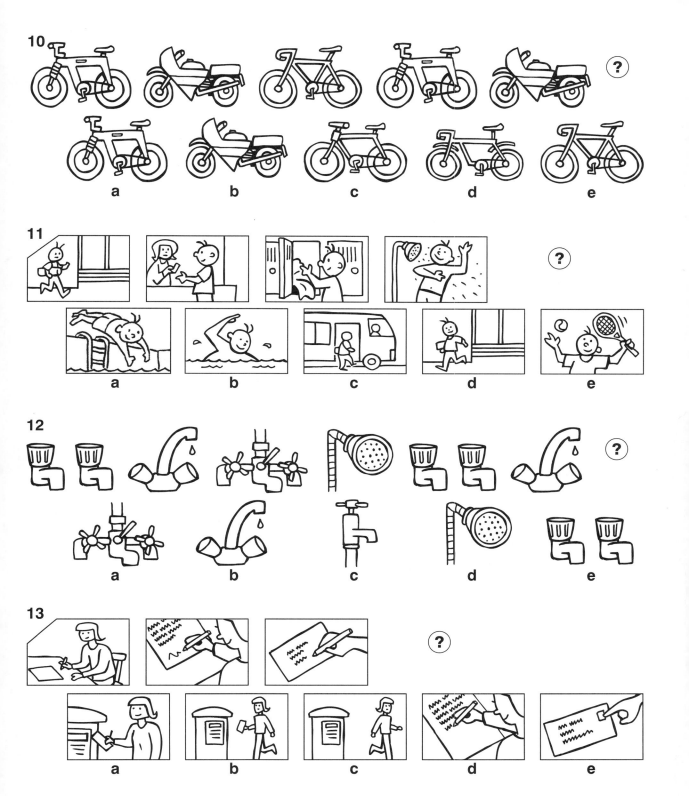

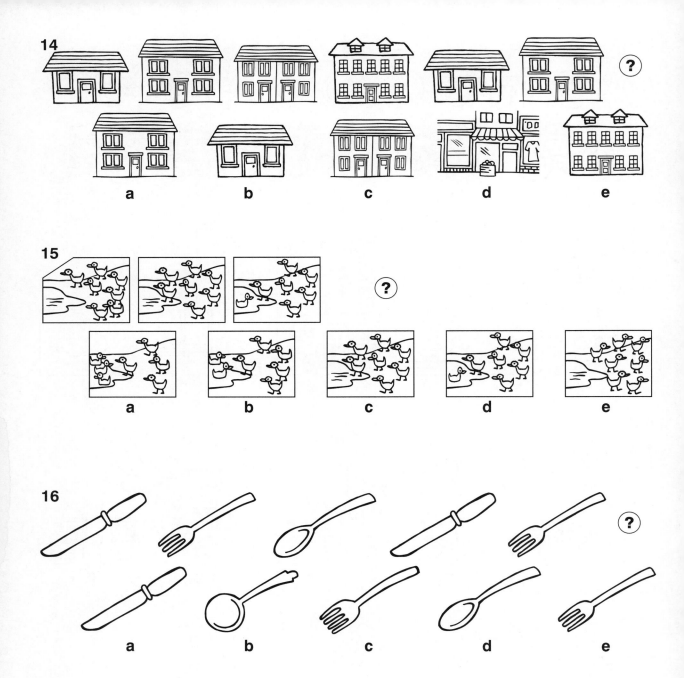

Which picture completes the second pair in the same way as the first pair?
Circle the letter.

Example

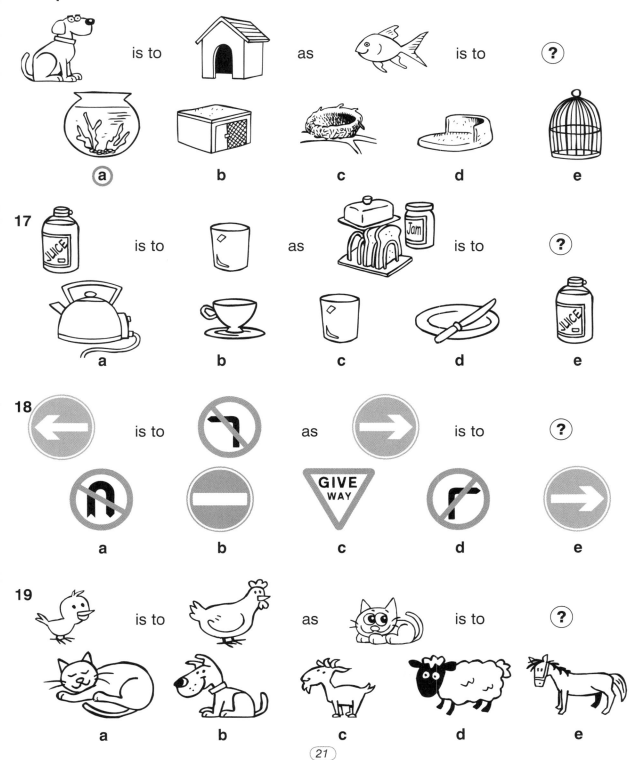

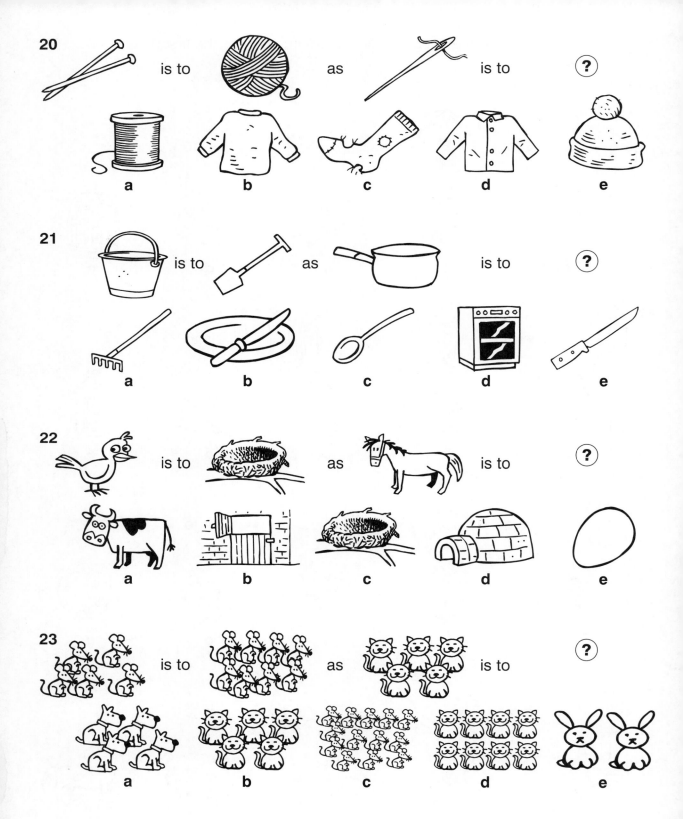

20 is to ... as ... is to ?

a   b   c   d   e

21 is to ... as ... is to ?

a   b   c   d   e

22 is to ... as ... is to ?

a   b   c   d   e

23 is to ... as ... is to ?

a   b   c   d   e

24

is to [tractor] as [astronaut in space] is to (?)

a [space shuttle]   b [moon in space]   c [cow]   d [alien]   e [train]

In which larger picture is the smaller picture hidden? Circle the letter.

Example

a   b   c   d   e

25

a   b   c   d   e

26

a   b   c   d   e

27

a   b   c   d   e

Which shape or picture completes the larger square? Circle the letter.

Example

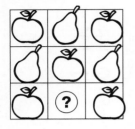

a

b

c

d

e

28

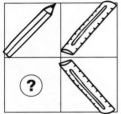

a

b

c

d

e

29

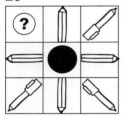

a

b

c

d

e

30

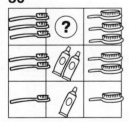

a

b

c

d

e

Now go to the Progress Chart to record your score! Total 30

Paper 4

Which is the odd one out? Circle the letter.

Example

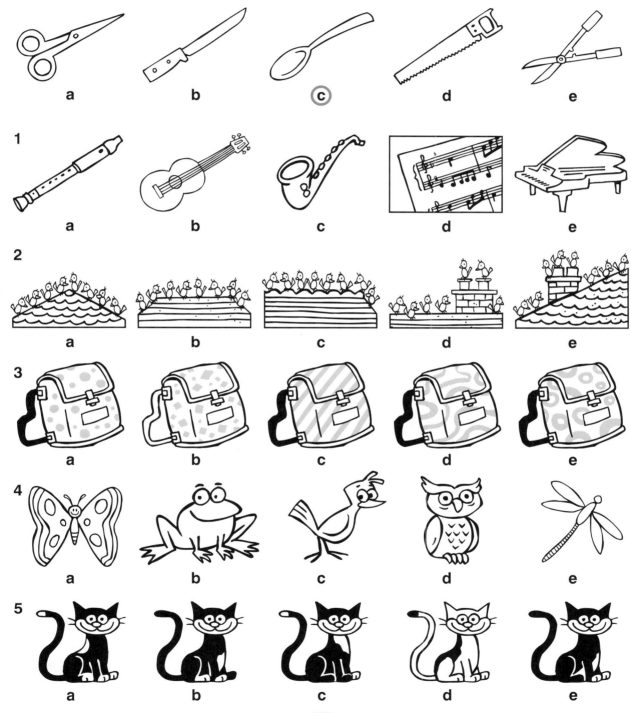

6

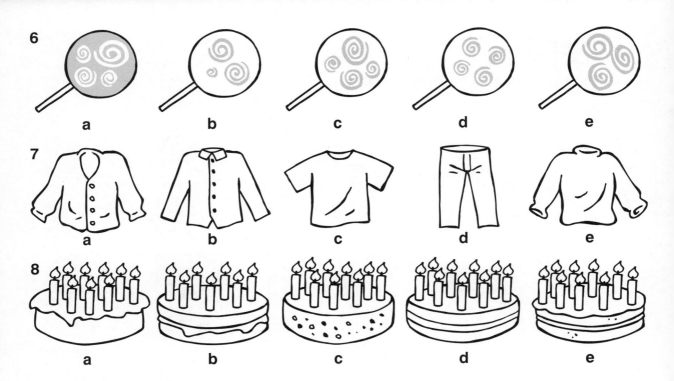

a   b   c   d   e

7

a   b   c   d   e

8

a   b   c   d   e

Which one comes next? Circle the letter.

Example

a   **b**   c   d   e

9

a   b   c   d   e

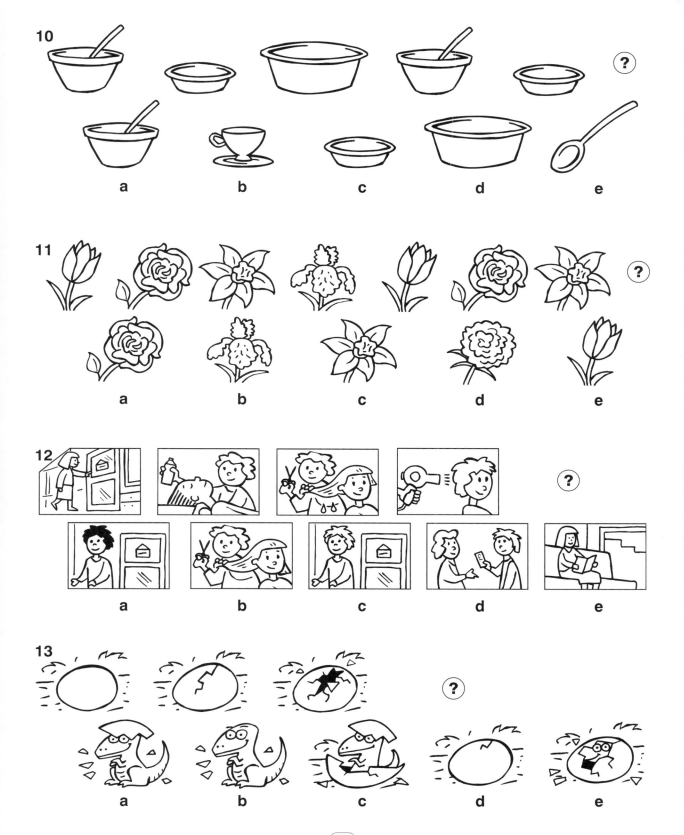

10

a   b   c   d   e

11

a   b   c   d   e

12

a   b   c   d   e

13

a   b   c   d   e

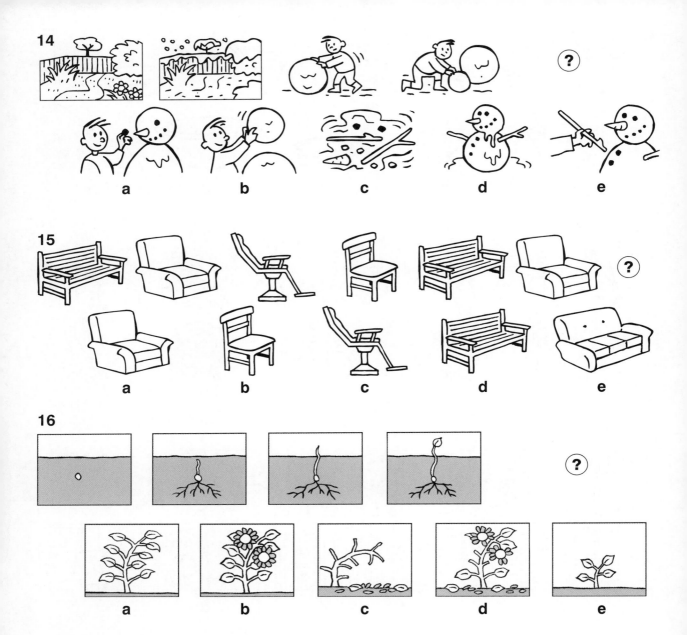

14

a b c d e

15

a b c d e

16

a b c d e

28

Which picture completes the second pair in the same way as the first pair?
Circle the letter.

Example

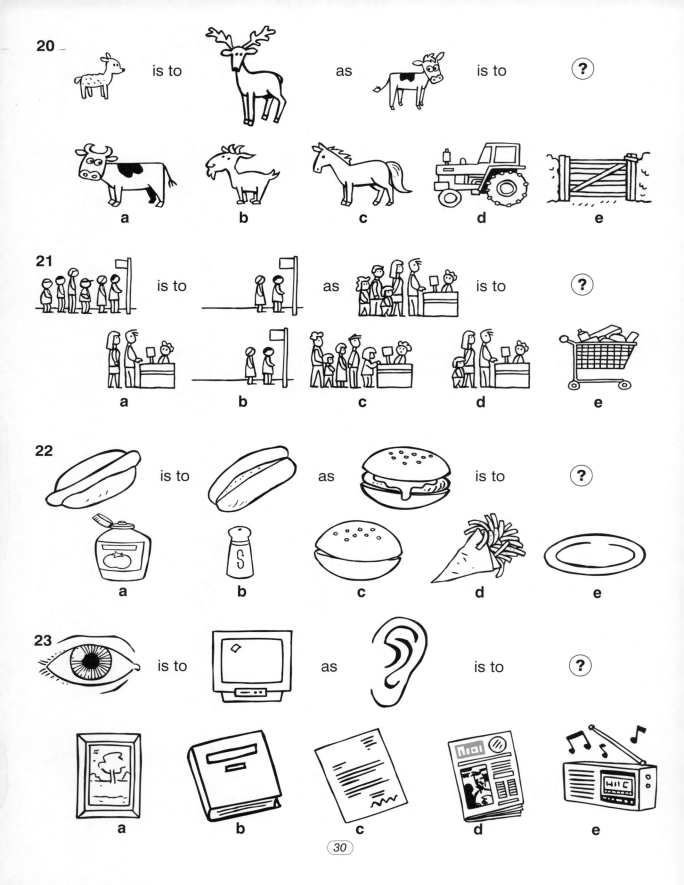

24

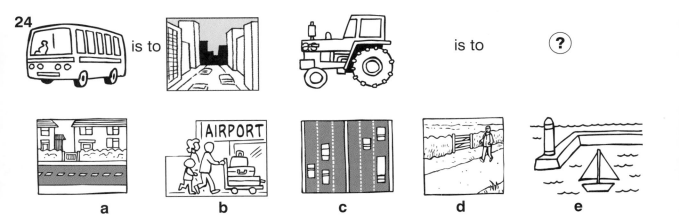

a   b   c   d   e

In which larger picture is the smaller picture hidden? Circle the letter.

Example

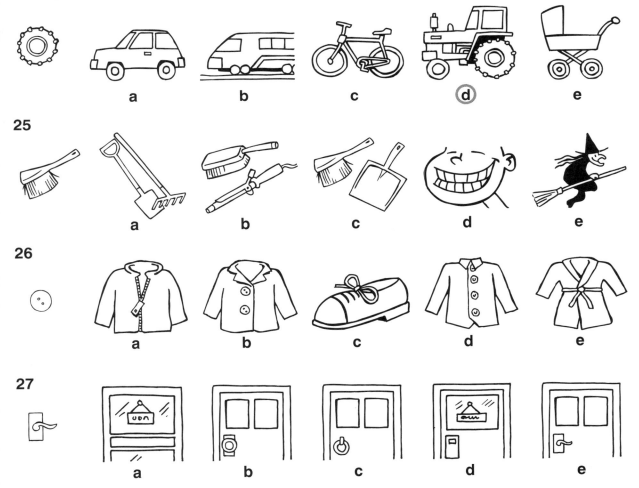

Which picture on the right is the reflection of the picture given on the left, in the dotted mirror line? Circle the letter.

Example

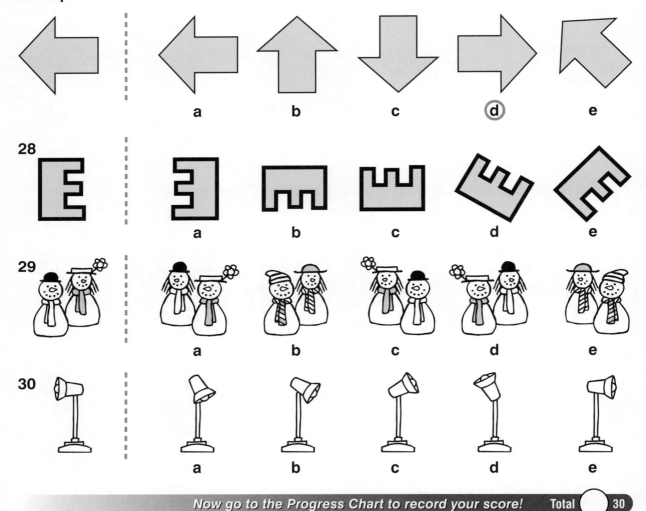

Now go to the Progress Chart to record your score!   Total ◯ 30

Paper 5

Which is the odd one out? Circle the letter.

Example

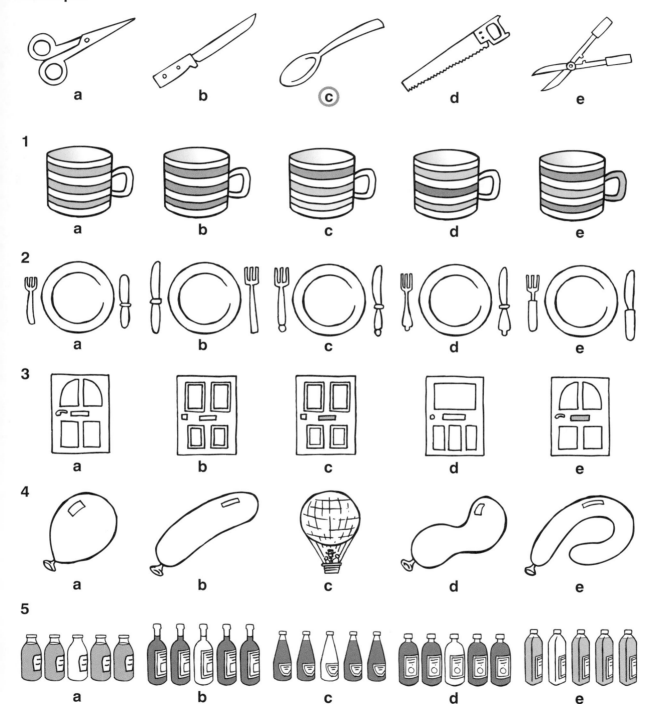

6

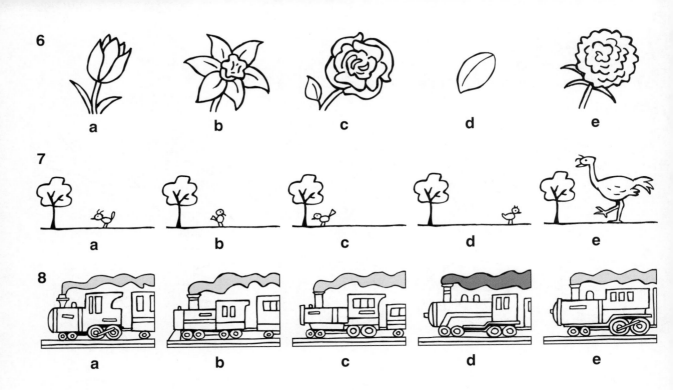

7

8

Which one comes next? Circle the letter.

Example

9

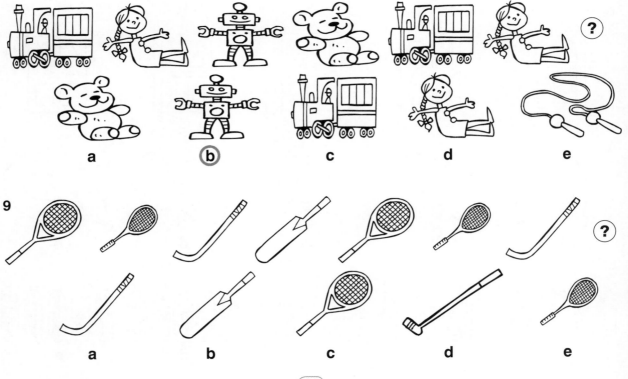

34

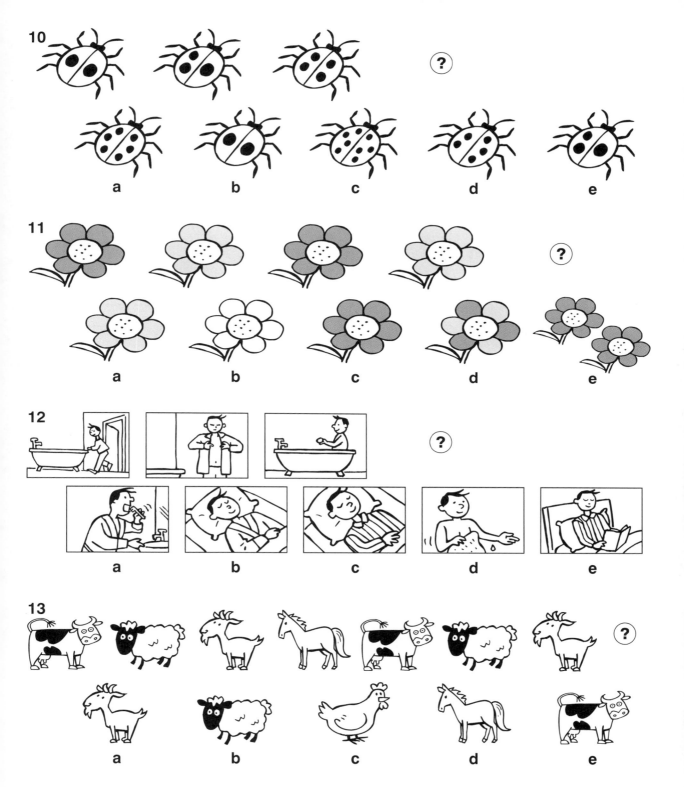

14

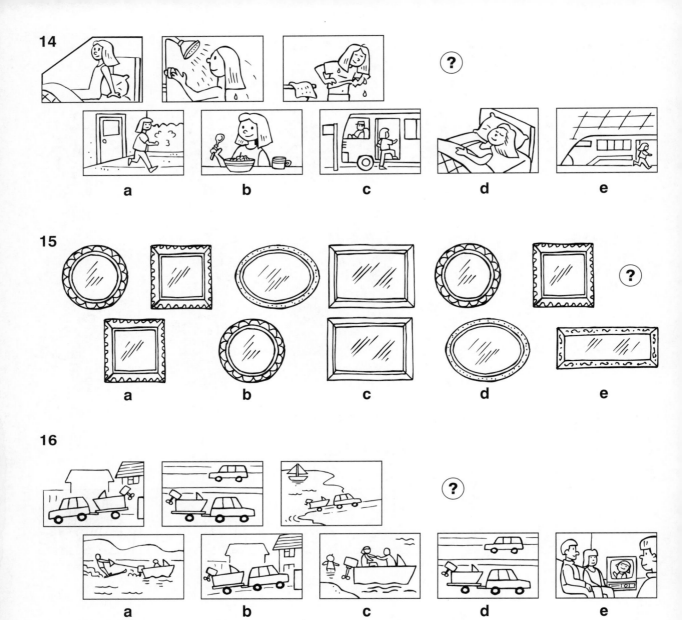

a   b   c   d   e

15

a   b   c   d   e

16

a   b   c   d   e

36

Which picture completes the second pair in the same way as the first pair?
Circle the letter.

Example

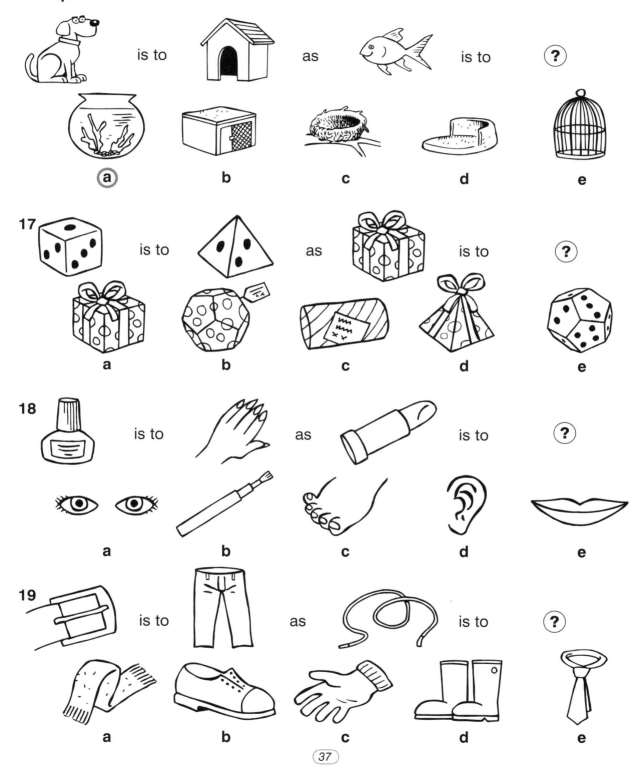

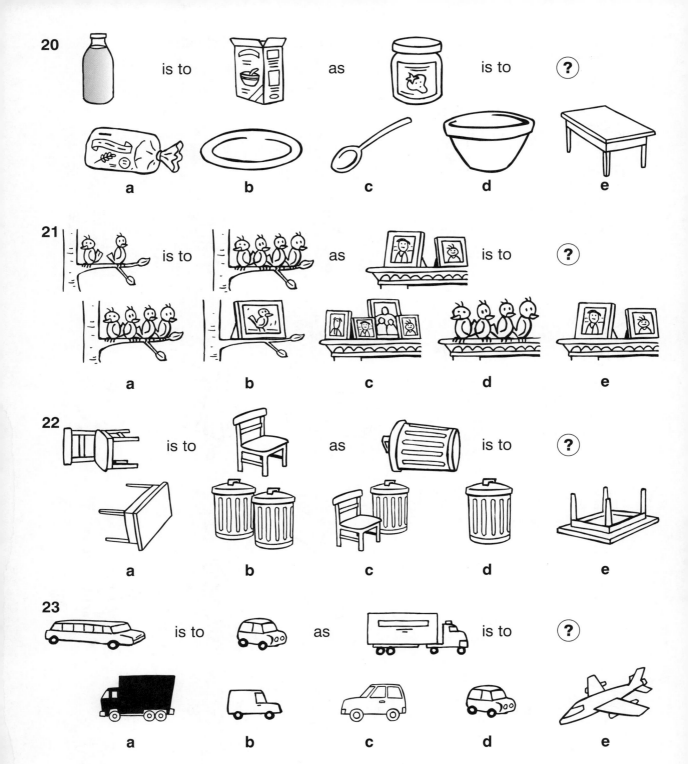

20 is to as is to ?

a b c d e

21 is to as is to ?

a b c d e

22 is to as is to ?

a b c d e

23 is to as is to ?

a b c d e

24

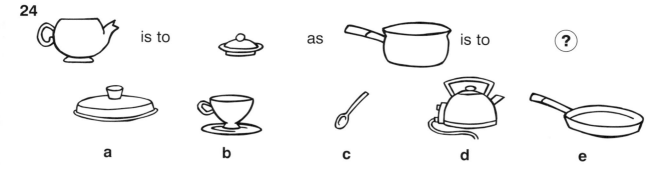

is to ☐ as ☐ is to (?)

a   b   c   d   e

Which picture on the right is the reflection of the picture given on the left, in the dotted mirror line? Circle the letter.

Example

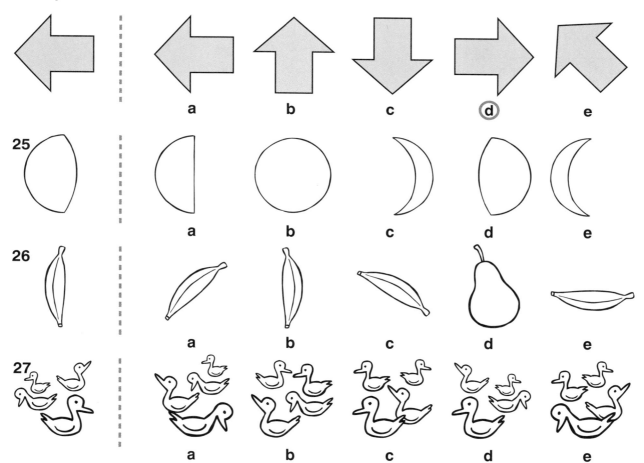

Which shape or picture completes the larger square? Circle the letter.

Example

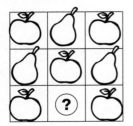

a

b

ⓒ

d

e

28

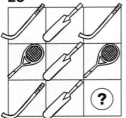

a

b

c

d

e

29

a

b

c

d

e

30

a

b

c

d

e

Now go to the Progress Chart to record your score!   Total 30

Paper 6

Which is the odd one out? Circle the letter.

Example

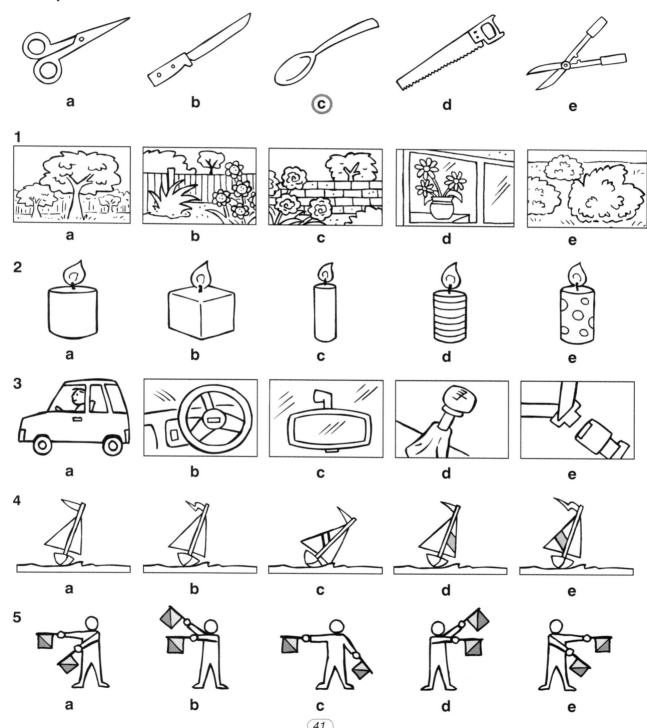

a   b   ⓒ   d   e

1

a   b   c   d   e

2

a   b   c   d   e

3

a   b   c   d   e

4

a   b   c   d   e

5

a   b   c   d   e

6

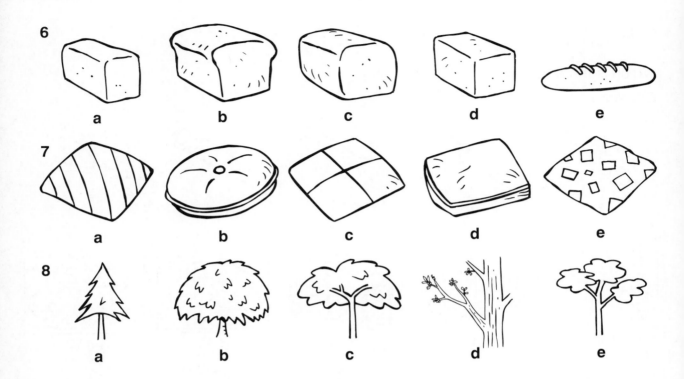

a   b   c   d   e

7

a   b   c   d   e

8

a   b   c   d   e

Which one comes next? Circle the letter.

Example

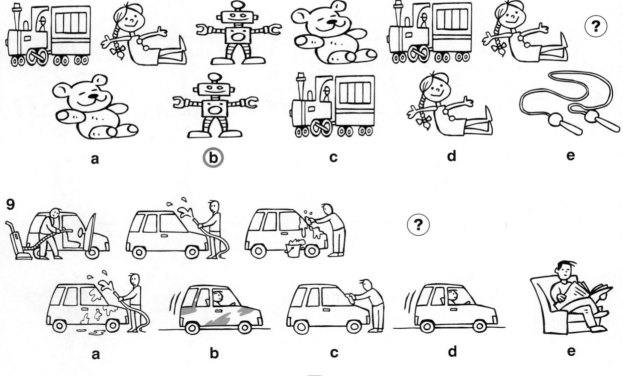

a   **b**   c   d   e

9

?

a   b   c   d   e

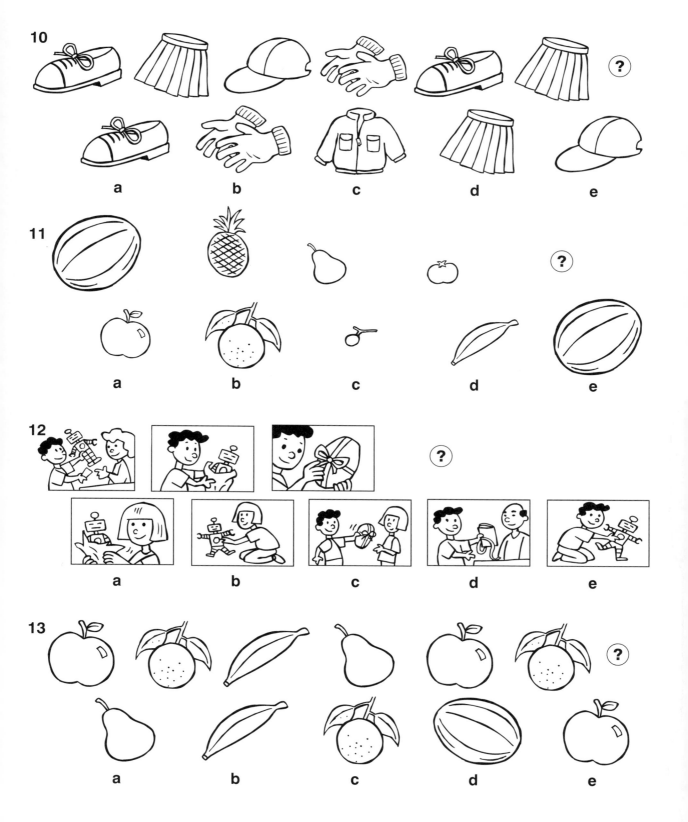

10

a b c d e

11

a b c d e

12

a b c d e

13

a b c d e

43

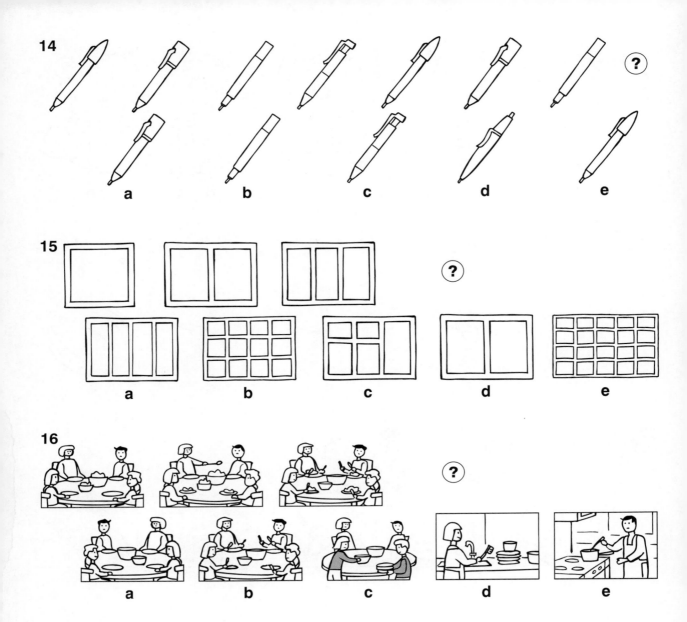

14

a b c d e

15

a b c d e

16

a b c d e

Which picture completes the second pair in the same way as the first pair?
Circle the letter.

Example

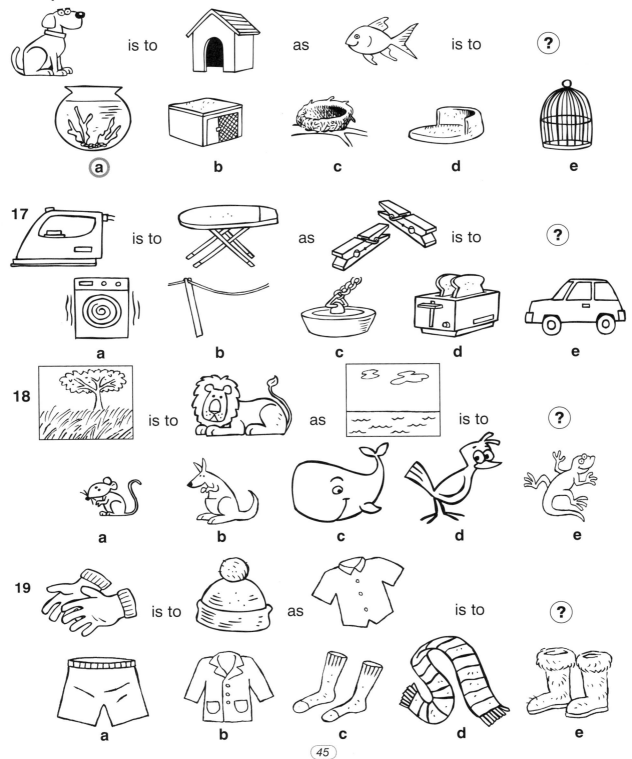

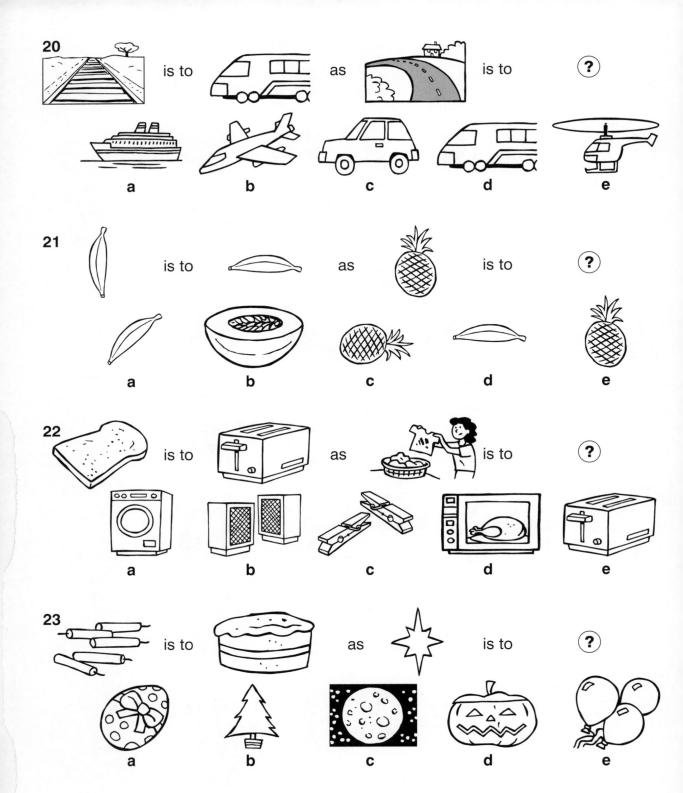

24

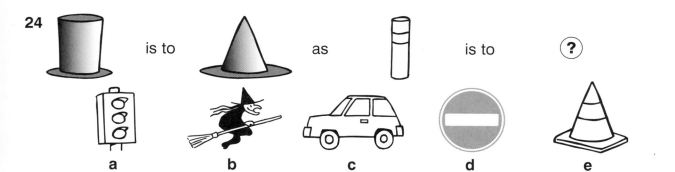

In which larger picture is the smaller picture hidden? Circle the letter.

Example

Which shape or picture completes the larger square? Circle the letter.

Example

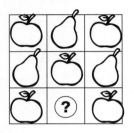

a   b   ⓒ   d   e

28

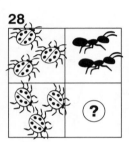

a   b   c   d   e

29

a   b   c   d   e

30

a   b   c   d   e

Now go to the Progress Chart to record your score!   Total ⬤ 30

Paper 7

Which is the odd one out? Circle the letter.

Example

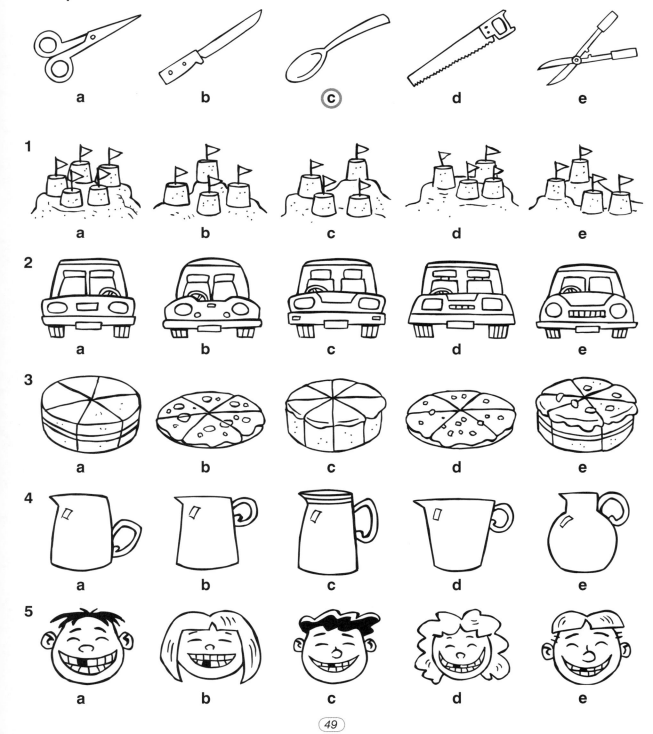

6

a   b   c   d   e

7

a   b   c   d   e

8

a   b   c   d   e

Which one comes next? Circle the letter.

Example

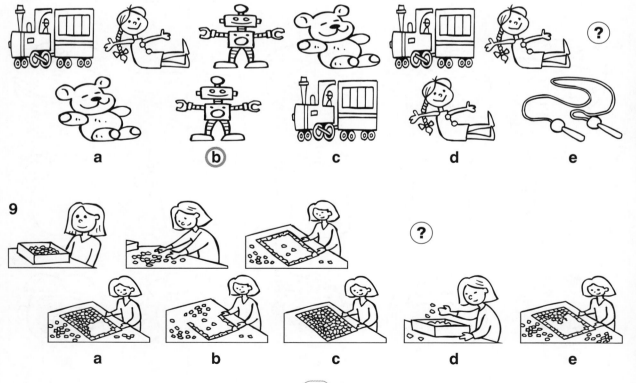

a   b   c   d   e

9

a   b   c   d   e

10

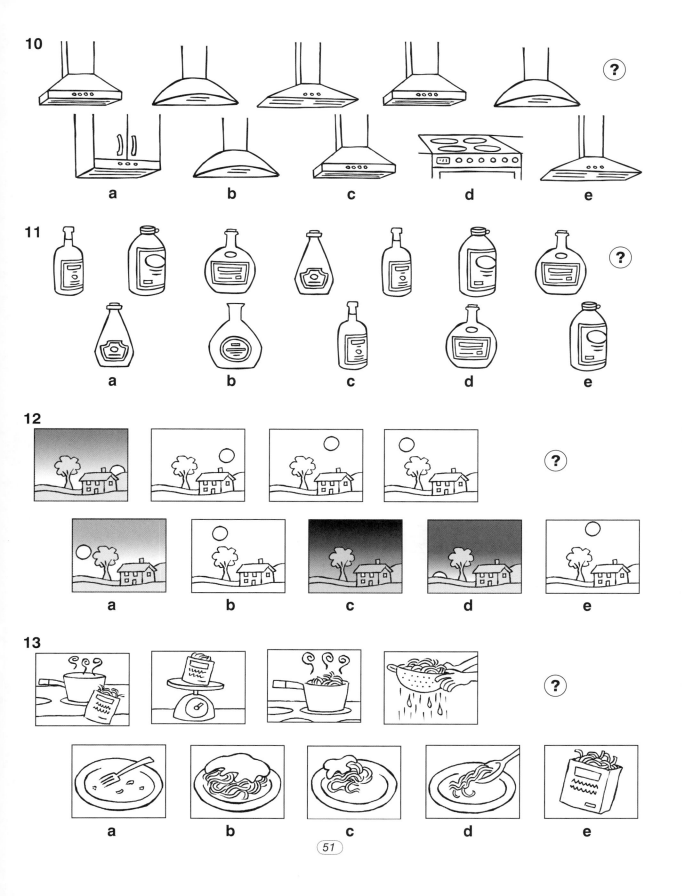

a   b   c   d   e

11

a   b   c   d   e

12

a   b   c   d   e

13

a   b   c   d   e

51

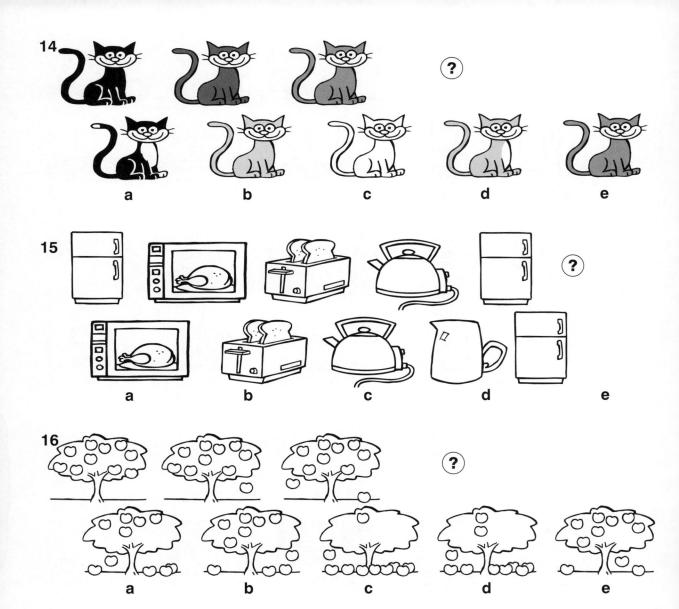

14

a b c d e

15

a b c d e

16

a b c d e

Which picture completes the second pair in the same way as the first pair?
Circle the letter.

Example

17

18

19

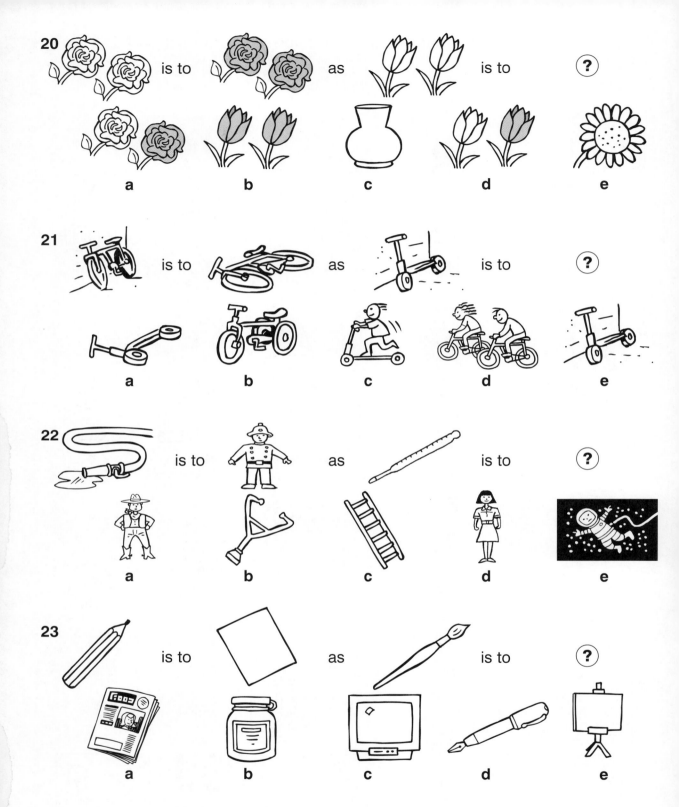

24

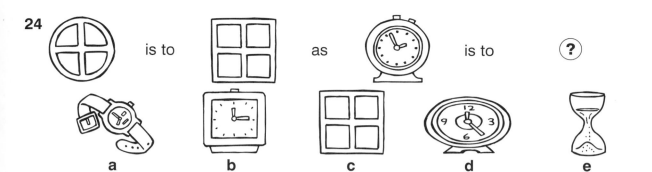

In which larger picture is the smaller picture hidden? Circle the letter.

Example

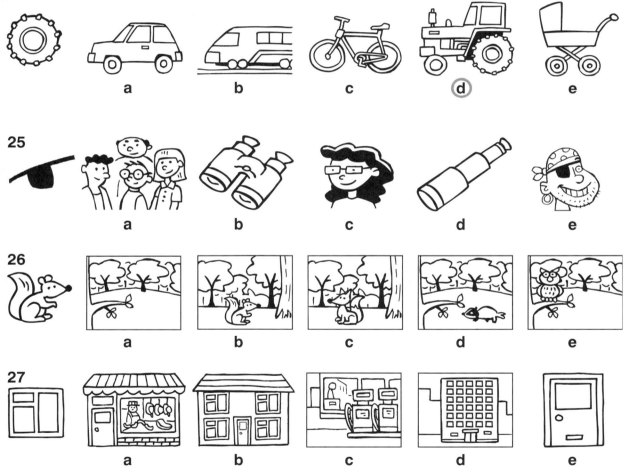

Which picture on the right is the reflection of the picture given on the left, in the dotted mirror line? Circle the letter.

Example

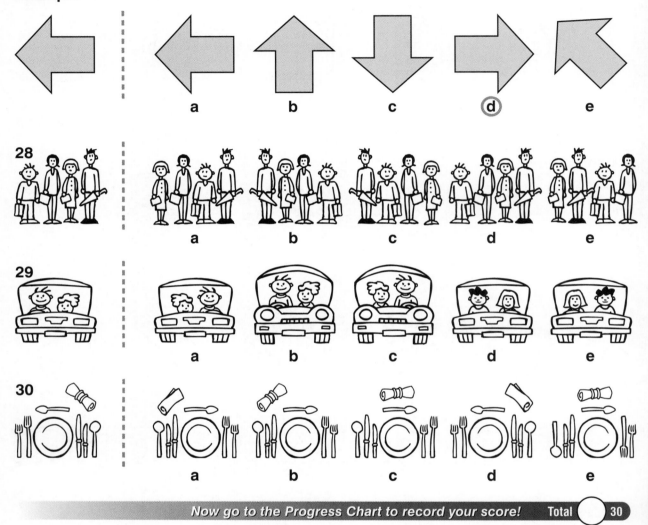

Paper 8

Which is the odd one out? Circle the letter.

Example

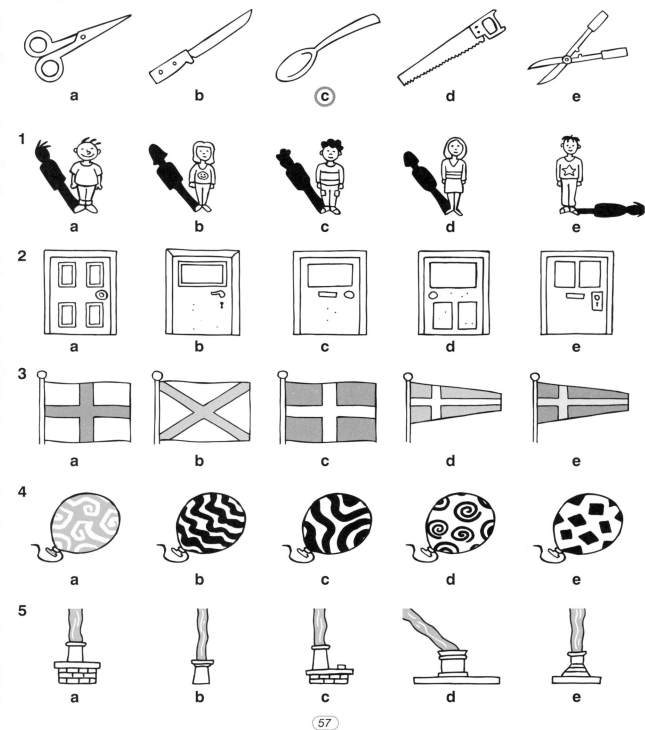

6

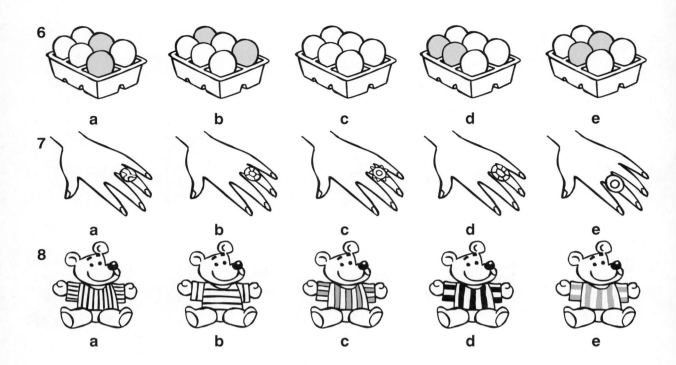

a   b   c   d   e

7

a   b   c   d   e

8

a   b   c   d   e

Which one comes next? Circle the letter.

Example

a   b   c   d   e

9

a   b   c   d   e

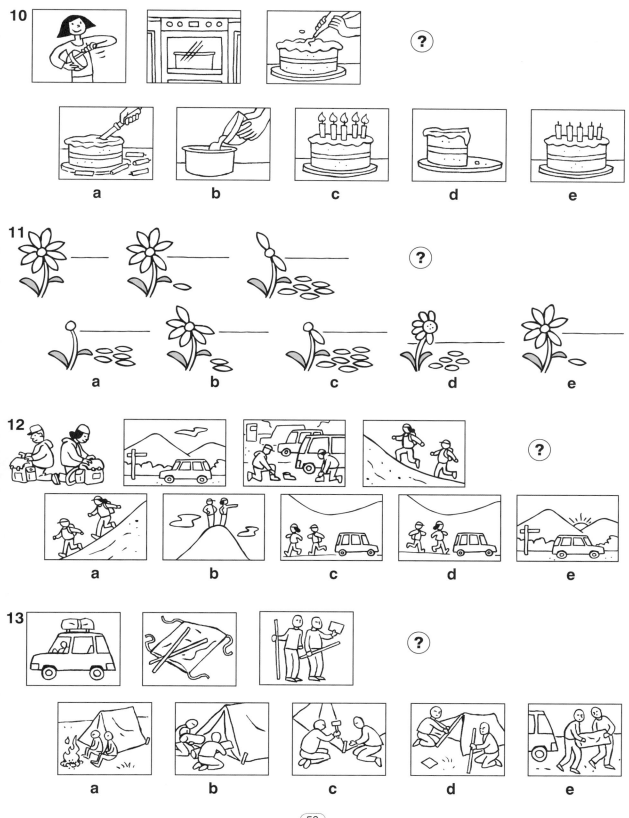

10

11

12

13

14

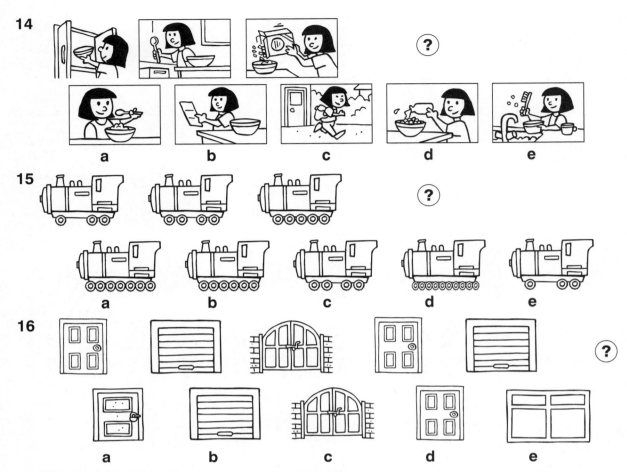

15

16

Which picture completes the second pair in the same way as the first pair?
Circle the letter.

Example

17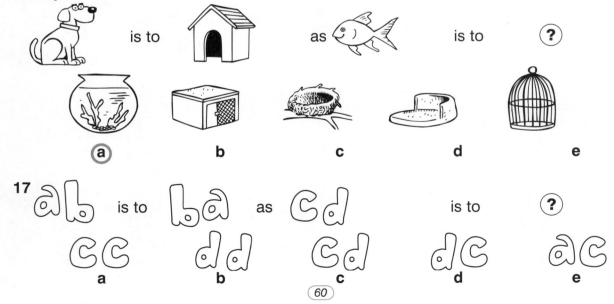

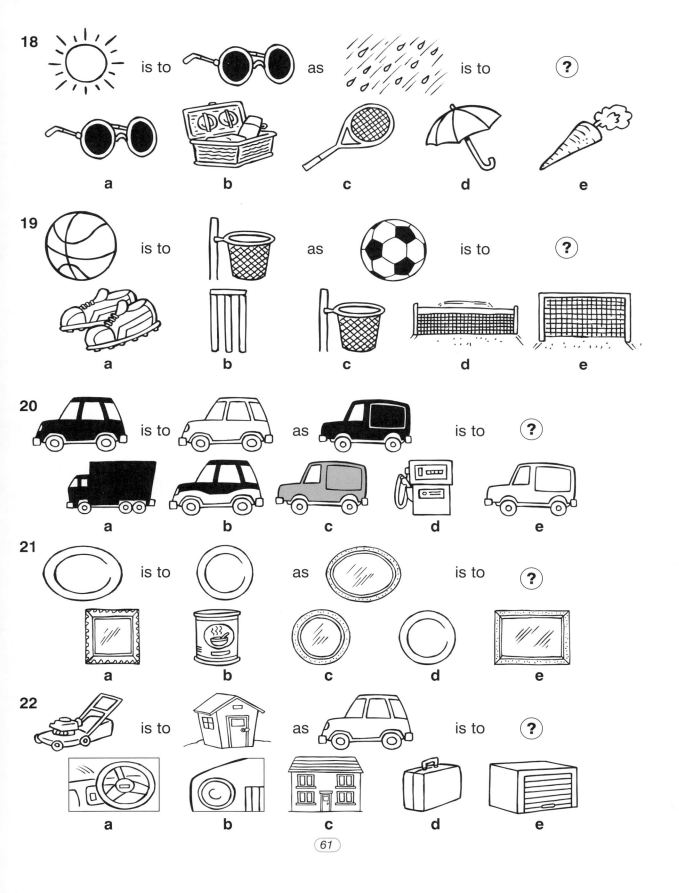

18 ☀ is to 🕶 as 🌧 is to **?**

a b c d e

19 🏀 is to 🗑 as ⚽ is to **?**

a b c d e

20 is to as is to **?**

a b c d e

21 is to as is to **?**

a b c d e

22 is to as is to **?**

a b c d e

23

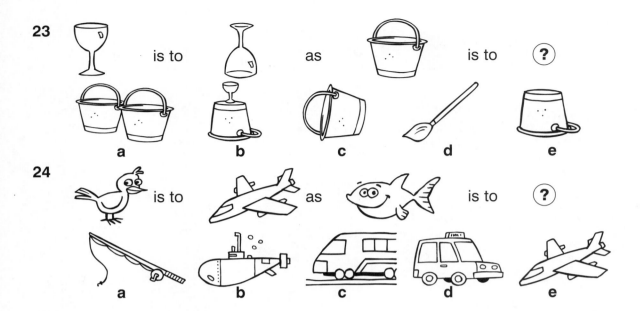

24

Which picture on the right is the reflection of the picture given on the left, in the dotted mirror line? Circle the letter.

Example

25

26

27

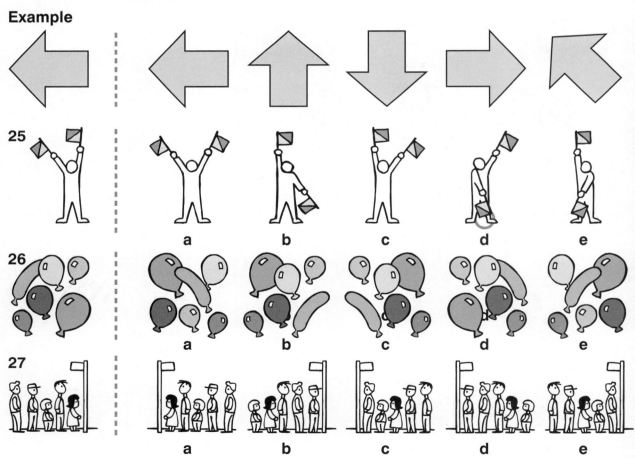

Which shape or picture completes the larger square? Circle the letter.

Example

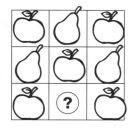
 a
 b
 ⓒ
 d
 e

28

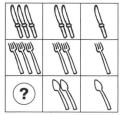
 a
 b
 c
 d
 e

29

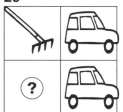
 a
 b
 c
 d
 e

30

 a
 b
 c
 d
 e

Now go to the Progress Chart to record your score! Total ◯ 30

Progress Chart   Non-verbal Reasoning 7 - 8 years

Total marks	Paper 1	Paper 2	Paper 3	Paper 4	Paper 5	Paper 6	Paper 7	Paper 8	Percentage
30									100%
27									90%
24									80%
21									70%
18									60%
15									50%
12									40%
9									30%
6									20%
3									10%
0									0%

Paper: 1, 2, 3, 4, 5, 6, 7, 8

Date ▶ 1 2.2.14

When you've finished the book read the Next Steps ➡